ACKNOWLEDGEMENTS

The authors would like to pay special tribute to the following people and organisations that have helped make this book possible:

John Hudson for editing and proof-reading the manuscript; Arran Heritage Museum, and in particular Archivist Stuart Gough for research and suggested corrections to the text, Dr Thomas Owen Clancy and Canongate Publishers for Agallamh na Senorach; Mrs Jean Humphries and Ruth and Alan Thompson for the excerpt from Machrie Moor, Steve Blamires for reading the text and suggesting additions, Mary Mackenzie and the Arran Federation S.W.R.I. for the excerpt from History of the Villages of the Isle of Arran and to the people of Arran for their kindness and hospitality over many years.

2nd edtion published April 2006
Copyright 2002 Allan Wright, Tony Bonning

ISBN10 0-9551143-3-0
ISBN13 978-0-9551143-3-5

Design by Wolffe and Co, Castle Douglas
Printed in Poland

published by Lyrical Scotland
an imprint of Cauldron Press Ltd

Parton House Stables
Castle Douglas
Kirkcudbrightshire
Scotland
DG7 3NB
Tel 01644 470260
Email info@lyricalscotland.com
www.lyricalscotland.com

Arran

By Allan Wright and Tony Bonning

The Isle of Arran from above Skipness, Kintyre

ARRAN

INTRODUCTION

There is, perhaps, no more beautiful sight than to stand on Ayr shore and watch the sun set into a cauldron of fire behind the jagged peaks of Arran. In Celtic legend there is a land away to the west called the Isles of the Blessed: it takes little stretch of the imagination to see Arran as such a place.

It is an island where the raw powers of Earth are vividly on show: from the mountain spires and ridges of the north to the great moorland plain of the south, and all ringed by a raised beach.

Although the great upheavals of far prehistoric times made their mark, it was the last Ice Age that brought the land near to its present structure. Glaciers gouged out the valleys and levelled the plains. As the ice withdrew northwards so hardier Arctic life forms, now found only atop the mountains, crept after it. Behind came a march of trees: first of the dwarf variety, birch and willow, then, gradually, mighty forests of pine, alder, ash, oak and hazel. With it came abundant wildlife and, in its wake, the nomadic hunter. Later came Neolithic then Bronze Age farmers whose chambered tombs, cairns and stone circles are testament to their passing. In its time Arran has seen the coming and going of Scots, Vikings and Normans. It has been populated, repopulated and, for one infamous period, depopulated.

Arran possesses an almost mythological attraction for those who live there and for those who visit, for it is a wondrous weave of the world's past and present: a place that, once visited, remains in the heart always.

Cir Mhor from Caisteal Abhail, "The Castles"

ARRAN

ICE AND FIRE

The first discernible view of Arran is of its northern mountains dominated by the almost pyramidal shape of Goat Fell. These granite masses were thrust up through the sedimentary strata as molten rock, or magma, 60 million years ago, when Scotland and Northern Ireland were still part of what is now North America. Arran was part of a string of volcanoes that ran from Skye to Antrim. Northern and southern Arran were themselves created from two of these natural furnaces.

Erosion wore away the northern volcano exposing the magma, which cooled as granite. The granite is of two forms, coarse and fine, with the former creating the dramatic tors and ridges of the mountaintops and the latter the more rounded hills of the lower ground. Granite itself is a composite rock formed from quartz, feldspar and mica giving it its distinctive sparkle. The granite boss is surrounded by Highland quartzite, which was formed from super-heated sandstone. Old red sandstone is another major feature of north Arran's geology and can be found along the String Road, which bisects the island, and more readily at Corrie where it is the significant feature of the shoreline. These sandstone features were created when Arran formed part of some ancient arid desert

Granite boulder, Pirates Cove, Corrie

There are two more granite intrusions in central and southern Arran, which together form the raised plateau of the south of the island. This area is mainly sandstone, but during the volcanic period magma was forced up and between the layers or cracks in the sandstone to form what are known as dykes. Prime examples of these are found along the southern shoreline looking for-all-the-world like man-made walls running out into the sea.

Glacial Boulders on the shore at Pirates Cove

Sunrise over Pladda and Ailsa Craig from Kildonan

During the series of Ice Ages which began 2.4 million years ago and ended some of 8,000 years ago, Arran and the rest of Scotland were occasionally covered in vast sheets of ice, sometimes kilometres deep. These moved southwards scouring the land, gouging out Kilbrannan Sound and the Firth of Clyde and distributing some of Arran's granite rocks, or erratics, as far as Galloway. Some 13,000 years ago the surrounding sea was 30 metres higher than at present creating what are termed raised beaches. The most recent raised beach of 6,000 years ago formed the flat area that rings the present-day island. The higher sea level is most obvious on the west coast where wave action has worn caves into the sandstone. The glaciers of 11,000 years ago put the final touch to Arran's geological architecture by gouging out her famed glens, creating her saw-toothed ridges and prominent coastal cliffs and distributing mountain debris or moraines across the low lying land.

Such is the diversity of geological features that Arran has chipped a unique niche for itself in the story of geology and has been a regular point of pilgrimage for aspiring geologists since Sir James Hutton, the *Father of Geology*, made his groundbreaking discoveries on the island in 1787.

Drumadoon Point

The Punchbowl at the summit of Cir Mhor with Jura in the distance

Rosa Water from Brodick Beach

FROM STONE CHIPS
TO MICROCHIPS

Stone Age

One can only make educated guesses at the drift of life back across the post-glacial landscape: Arctic life followed by the wildwood. Migrating forests of pine, oak, alder, elm and hazel populated by boar, bear and marten; rivers and lochs teeming with salmon, beaver and wildfowl and the hills running with wolf and reindeer. About 8,000 years ago, Mesolithic or Middle-Stone-Age hunter-gatherers moved across the continental land-bridge that joined Britain to Europe and up the east coast of England, crossing to the Clyde by way of river valleys such as the Tweed or Forth. The main diet of these early nomads was probably shellfish, due to its all-year-round ease of collection. It is quite probable that these early colonists crossed to Arran over Kilbrannan Sound.

Lower Falls, Glenashadale

Glenrosa Water from below The Saddle

Upper Falls, Glenashadale

Relic millstones by the stones, Machrie Moor

The first true settlers, Neolithic farmers, arrived on Arran over 5,000 years ago. In those days the entire population of Scotland may have numbered only in the hundreds. The whole of Arran, except for the high mountain slopes, would have been covered in woodland and scrub so, as growers of cereals and keepers of domesticated animals, the people would have begun a process of *slash and burn* to create cereal fields and pasture. On and around the triangulated plain of Machrie Moor is known to have been the chosen location for these agricultural people. The Moor was extensively cultivated through the Bronze Age up to the Iron Age of the Celts 2,500 years ago, when climatic changes brought wetter and cooler weather. A consequent blanket of peat effectively prevented cultivation but, to our benefit, has acted as a biological library of these times.

Stone circle, Machrie Moor

On the Atlantic margin from the Algarve to the north of Norway there are over 40,000 known chambered tombs, cairns and circles of stone. These are the monuments of humanity who had migrated at the pace of the herd from Asia Minor until they had met the seemingly insurmountable barrier of the great ocean. Here they made their indelible mark. Arran, and in particular Machrie Moor, can claim to be one of the most important of all these sites.

The significance of any megalithic site is open to debate, but there is much evidence to suggest that they are associated with death and rebirth. It is almost certain that the people of these times had not disassociated from nature but saw themselves as part of the great whole of life. Time was not seen as linear but rather in cycles. The stars spun around Cynosure, the Pole Star, the sun and moon circled the heavens. All life rose out of the underworld reached skyward only to return to the womb of the Earth. Somehow these sites reflected that belief. Regardless of any and all views, no one can visit any of these sites without coming away touched by a sense of wonder, a respect for people at the very frontiers of existence who took time to create marvels that still fill us with awe.

Machrie Bay from King's Cave trail

Wildflowers, West Coast

In the fresh of morning we stood beside them there

In the wide bowl of the hills, with heather, harebells

Buttercups, ling, meadowsweet, rushes, stretching

Away to the high sharp line, clear in the early light

Of peaks eternally silent, immovable; they

Silent, immovable too, great fangs of stone

Erect, grey-brown, sharp against sky's blue vault.

Machrie Moor (Excerpt)
Professor Arthur Humphreys

Three stones, Machrie Moor

Standing Stone at Druid, Auchencar

Solitary Stone near Moss Farm, Machrie Moor

Iron Age

Although Scotland as a whole has seen numerous invasions, change was always gradual. Often as not, trade was the first point of contact. The coming of the warrior Celts (Picts then Britons) during the Iron Age rung changes that were already in progress. The increasing presence of warrior cultures brought about the creation of forts and duns. There are fifteen such sites on Arran, the most prominent being at Drumadoon near Blackwaterfoot, North Glen Sannox and King's Cross Point. It is more than likely that these fortified homesteads were used right up to medieval times, if not later. The fact that iron rusts whereas bronze does not means that archaeological material from the later and more sophisticated Iron Age is, ironically, less available than the earlier Bronze Age. This has resulted in major gaps in available knowledge about Arran from 500BC to 500AD.

In the sixth-century south-west Scotland saw the arrival of christianised Celts or Scots from the north of Ireland. Argyll along with Arran was forged into the kingdom of Dalriada.

From atop "the doon fort" to the King's Caves

King's Cross Fort and Holy Isle

Arran of the many deer,
  ocean touching its shoulders
island where troops are ruined,
  ridge where blue spears are blooded.

High above the sea its summit,
  clear its green growth, rare its bogland;
blue island of glens, of horses,
  of peaked mountains, oaks and armies.

Frisky deer on its mountains,
  moist bogberries in its thickets,
cold waters in its rivers,
  acorns on its brown oak-trees.

Hunting dogs and keen greyhounds,
  brambles, sloes of dark blackthorn;
close against the woods its dwellings;
  stags sparring in its oak-groves.

Purple lichen from its rocks,
  faultless grass on its greenswards;
on its crags, a shielding cloak;
  fawns capering, trout leaping.

Smooth its plains, well-fed its swine,
  glad its fields - believe the story! -
nuts upon its hazels' tops,
  the sailing of longships past it.

Fine for them when good weather comes-
  trout beneath its river banks;
gulls reply round its white cliff-
  fine at all times is Arran.

Agallamh na Senorach (excerpt)
The Discussions of the Old Men (12th century)
Translation: Thomas Owen Clancy

Glen Sannox

SAINTS AND SINNERS

Whiting Bay beach

In Medieval times Religious hermits and missionary monks visited Arran and established cells for religious meditation. This cell or *kil* was the focal point for religious observance by the local population. Gradually the word was adopted to mean church, hence Kildonan or Kilpatrick.

According to the folklore of Arran, the most famous of her religious sons was Molaise, who may have been the St Molaise who died in 639AD at Leithglinn Monastery in the west of Ireland. Molaise from the gaelic *mo*, meaning, my or my dear, and *las*, meaning, light, is reputed to have sought refuge in a shallow cave on Holy Island; thus giving it its old name of Eilan na Molaise, pronounced eye-lan na mowli-shi. The stepping-off point for the Holy Isle on the main island was eventually, through language corruption, called Lamlash. The Tibetan Buddhist Monastery at Eskdalemuir, in the Scottish Borders is maintaining the religious tradition of this sanctuary through its fairly recent acquisition of the island.

Kilpatrick Point, Blackwaterfoot

Lamlash, meadow and Holy Isle

Holy Isle profile from Corrie shore

In the 8th century, fearless freebooters sailed from the coast of Norway and into history. Crossing the northern sea the Vikingr, derived from *vik*, the Norse word for a bay, invaded and dominated the Shetland and Orkney Islands and northern part of Scotland, which they renamed Southland or Sutherland. From here they sailed to the Western Isles and established their sovereignty there before moving down the west coast of Scotland. Their first recorded assault on the relatively peaceful kingdom of Dalriada was in 794AD, when they sacked Iona. Over a period of four hundred years the Vikingr intermarried with the Celtic people of the Western Isles and eventually adopted their language. In time they held sovereignty over the Western Isles Argyll, Galloway, the Isle of Man and the east of Ireland. A new name was eventually attached to them, the Gallghaidhel or Stranger Gaels.

From Mullach Beag, Holy Isle, to Claughlands Point

Bhudda Painting, Holy Isle

By the middle of the 12th century the Gallghaidhel had established a semi-autonomous domain under the leadership of Somerled, Lord of the Isles; though the Western Isles remained under the overlordship of the king of Norway and the mainland territories under the King of Scotland. It was the disputed ownership of Kintyre, Arran and Bute that led to the fateful Battle of Largs, where Alexander III of Scotland defeated the Norwegian, King Hakon, in 1263. Runic inscriptions, reputedly from that time, are still to be found in St Molaise cave on Holy Isle. In 1266 all of Scotland including Arran and the Western Isles came under suzerainty of the Scottish crown.

Brodick Castle from Rose Garden

Ancient Scotland's ownership was based on communal or tribal lines. By the middle of the 12th century, Scotland had come under Norman influence and feudalism introduced. Land and the common man had become political pawns and the lands of Arran fared no better or worse than elsewhere. In the wake of the Battle of Largs, and the purchase of the West from the crown of Norway, the Norman, Alexander, High Steward of Scotland, claimed Arran, by virtue of his marriage to a granddaughter of Somerled. During the invasion of Edward Longshanks in 1296 the island was granted to another Norman, Thomas Bysset. The Byssets were later given the task of stamping out the followers of a Norman turncoat, one Robert de Bruis.

On his return from exile on Rathlin Island off the coast of Ireland, de Bruis used Arran as a stepping stone for his return to the mainland in 1307. According to the great narrative poem, *The Bruce*, written in 1375 by the Archdeacon of Aberdeen, John Barbour (a man who had known survivors of the Wars of Independence), two of de Bruis's lieutenants, Sir James Douglas and Sir Robert Boyd, made an attack on the garrison at Brodick Castle. Unable to overthrow the castle, they retreated to a stronghold in a glen. Recent work by the water board has uncovered numerous archaeological sites around the island. Among them was a corner of a building that some have suggested might be the very place.

Brodick Castle from Brodick Beach

Lochranza Castle from Colliemore

Following the traditions of his Norman ancestors, Bruce is reputed have granted land charters on Arran. It is a known fact that his grandson continued the tradition by granting lands to the Fullarton family. The Menteiths who had supported Edward against Bruce were also granted Lochranza Castle by marrying into the Bruce family.

In the 15th century the Stewarts were again associated with Arran, and Kildonan Castle in particular. Lochranza was granted to the Montgomeries, in the hope that they would keep at bay the continuing ravages of the Lords of Isles. Shortly afterwards Sir Thomas Boyd, a descendant of the intrepid Sir Robert, was made Earl of Arran. Falling into disgrace he was replaced by James Hamilton, whose family has been associated with Arran right up to recent times.

Lochranza Bay

Monyquil Farm and Ben Nuis

Feral goat, Holy Isle

In the way of things, it is only the names of semi-legendary saints, lords and heroes that come down to us from the past. It would appear that common humanity lies unremembered. Yet, while we have no tag for them, the fact is their imprint is all about us: cleared forests, dykes and ditches, tracks and quarries. Even the fortresses, tombs and holy places, though built for those saints, lords and heroes, were cut, dragged and piled up by the hand of common humanity. As to living conditions of ordinary people: there would have been little to tell the difference between the habitation and the lifestyle of Neolithic farming communities and the clachans of the 19th century. The twenty five metre long, rectangular blackhouses were little different from the circular houses of five thousand years ago, in that they were dry-stone constructions, in-filled with sod or clay, with timber roof supports covered by thatched straw or heather. The diet was probably much the same: mainly oatmeal in its various disguises and occasional cheese, fish and goat flesh. The one difference would have been the potato.

Up until the clearances in the early 19th century, community life was based around the clachan or fermtoun - the present-day towns and villages largely did not exist before then. While the aristocracy performed their power plays, pressed menfolk into military service and inflicted taxes, people got on with their meagre subsistence. Farming was largely a communal effort based on strip farming or runrig, an inefficient system that was bound to change with new developments in agriculture in the late 18th century. While a number of innovative schemes were employed, they largely failed and had the effect of tearing apart the old communities. Regardless of the ethics of land clearance, evolution was inevitable: times changed, the world moved on and Arran with it. Apart from the copious flocks of sheep, the island was once again, *Arran of the many deer.*

Tigheanfraoch Farm, North Feorline

Whiting Bay and Holy Isle

SEA, FOREST, MOOR AND MOUNTAIN

It is often said of Arran that it is Scotland in miniature. A cliché perhaps, but, like most clichés, is apt. It has highland to the north and upland and lowland to the south: the difference is that it has sea on all sides. Though not a distant island, it has, at least in the past, needed to be largely self-sufficient. Agriculture was restricted to the band of raised beach strung about the island, but the sea was a seemingly limitless resource.

From the most ancient of times, crossing land was a tiring and hazardous prospect, so people travelled by the coastlines, and familiarity with the sea became second nature. Even in Bronze Age times, the sea was the equivalent of today's roads and motorways, and sea travel the norm. People from the Mediterranean traded right up to Scotland (and no doubt vice versa), so it is hardly surprising that foreign artefacts have been found in the graves of that time.

Until recently the Firth of Clyde was a rich source of fish: cod, whiting, haddock, flounder and sole as well as lobster and crab. In the middle of the 19th century, almost one hundred fishing boats plied their trade from the island. By the early 20th century, this had all but ceased. The island was also a rich source of seamen and the quality of Arran sailors renowned. From the late 18th century until the middle 19th century the smuggling of Arran Water was an honoured, if dangerous, pastime.

Aside from a few part-time lobster fishers, the RNLI and the Brodick and Lochranza ferries, the islands' great tradition of the sea is no more.

Lochranza – Claonaig ferry at Lochranza

From Meall Mor, above Glen Catacol

Summit of Goat Fell and North Goat Fell

Climatic changes and the requirements of an agricultural society - the need for fire for heat, cooking and the production of metal tools and weapons - means that the blanket of forest that once covered Arran is now all but gone. Though the landscape of a hundred years ago was largely bare and exposed moorland and mountain, local wood was still being used for boatbuilding. The famous bobbins or pirns that gave Pirnmill its name were being shaped from local timber until supply ran out in 1840. In recent times the Forestry Commission has reforested many parts of the island with alien softwoods. Regardless of feelings, the woodlands are there and provide work on an island with little in the way of homegrown industry. Commission policy now includes the need for environmentally sensitive planting, including native hardwoods, which can only bode well for the future.

No visit to Arran would be complete without at least an attempt to climb Goat Fell. At 874 metres, it is the highest peak on the island and provides a spectacular view. From the summit one can see the top of the Merrick in Galloway, Ailsa Craig, Antrim in the north of Ireland, Kintyre and right up past the Isle of Bute to Ben Lomond and the Highlands. Inbye are Arran's own magnificent peaks of Beinn Tarsuinn, Cir Mhor and Caisteal Abhail and, away to the West, Beinn Bharrain and Beinn Bhreac: mountains that are unsurpassed anywhere in the world for beauty and grandeur.

The ascent of Goat Fell

SOWING THE SEEDS OF CIVILISATION

Domestication of livestock and the cultivation of crops began in Asia Minor 10,000 years ago. The spread of farming culture from there would have been a combination of natural expansion through increased population, migration from drought and pestilence or fleeing from invaders. It would still take another 4,500 years before reaching the shores of Arran.

Original farming was a '*slash and burn*' process, working the ground until it was worn out, then moving to a new site. Any manure was from domesticated animals. Later people would discover the fertilising properties of seaweed and rotational methods of farming, but it was still a hit and miss affair.

Two hundred years ago, in the community based farming system of the clachans, there were two cultivated areas: the *infields* next to the clachan that were cultivated annually, and the *outfields*, which were grazed, cropped, then left fallow. Crops were: cereals, peas, beans and potatoes with flax grown for clothing.

Open strip farming, or runrig, was the chosen method, and ground allocated, usually by the drawing of lots. Small black cattle were reared for milk and cheese and then, along with horses, exported to the mainland. Goats, sheep and poultry were also raised for home use. Poor agricultural technique meant that life was usually at a subsistence level.

Ruined croft, An Torr

Spring Lambs at the Barking House, Lochranza

Pladda and Ailsa Craig from Ballymeanoch, Kildonan

As late as 1874 a Mr. Mitchell says of Arran, "The people live in barbarous looking huts, in many cases a but and ben," and goes on to say that the ruling family were responsible for this thing. The small farmers were not allowed to improve their houses. That is quite true, as I can well remember. Common decency could not be preserved under these conditions. I know of a case of where a death and a birth happened in the same house at the same time under these conditions. It is exceedingly difficult to restrain one's language when at the same time the landlord himself had some of the finest mansions in the realm.

CLANS OF SHISKINE
PAST AND PRESENT
Compiled and read by
Mr. Charles Robertson, Burncliff, Shiskine, to the Natives
of Arran in Glasgow, March, 1936

Cottage by Largybeg

Change came in the early 19th century, resulting in the clearances, bigger farms, enclosed fields and sheep on the hills. Initial changes were disastrous in every way, but by the 20th century, farming had become a stabilised practice and as good as anywhere else, with Arran cheese having a deserved worldwide reputation.

In the agricultural sphere, Arran is best known for its potatoes. The hobby of one man, Donald McKelvie, an Arran shopkeeper, who, from 1901 until 1945, bred some of the most famous names of the humble tattie: Arran Victory, Arran Banner and Arran Pilot. The most popular British potato, Maris Piper, was bred from the 1932 Gold Medal winner, Arran Cairn.

RING, STRING, ROSS AND CROSSING FROM ARDROSSAN

The development of roads and transport aided integration of the island's communities and, in turn, allowed ease of trade with the mainland. Nowadays, with a car, one can catch a ferry and cross to Arran in an hour, then leisurely circumnavigate the island's 56 miles in less than two hours, or cross from east to west in thirty minutes. In the 18th century, travel was by foot or horse on bridle paths and drove roads, or by boat. At the beginning of the 19th century, road-building began in earnest, starting with a properly surfaced track suitable for wheeled vehicles between Lamlash and Brodick. By the middle of the century, a road circled the island with two crossing inland: the Ross from Lamlash to Sliddery and the String from Cladach, just north of Brodick, to Blackwaterfoot: the latter surveyed by the famed Thomas Telford. The String posed a particular problem for wheeled vehicles due to the steep incline out of Cladach. In 1909 Colin (Col) Currie of Ballymichael, a horse-drawn carrier and postman, ingeniously convinced local people to part with their old boots and shoes. These he kept in a pile at his stable in Shedog for placing between the brake-block and the wheel when descending. People still added to the pile long after the service had ceased and the heap was a landmark for a further twenty years. Legend has it that when the rustic Col appeared at the Albion works in Glasgow in 1912 and asked to buy a motorised charabanc, the staff, perhaps deciding to humour the Arranach, enquired how he expected to pay the £650. Col promptly drew a wad of notes from his pocket and counted off the amount.

Ben Tarsuin and Cir Mhor from Cnoc Dubh

The Postbox by Glaister Bridge, The String

One of the unique features of Arran's roads is the series of stones that grace every mile. Numbered from Old Brodick and running clockwise round the island, and from east to west on the Ross and String roads, these small triangular sandstone columns have the miles engraved on the top shield-like surface.

Inevitably, boats played a significant part in the history and life of Arran. In the days before roads the quickest way to travel from Lochranza in the north to Kildonan in the south was by boat. Travel to and from the island had, of course, to be by this means. As to an actual ferry service: the first ran from Saltcoats to Brodick in 1770. With the coming of steam navigation, packet services became reliable and more frequent. In 1840 the railway system reached the purpose-built harbour at Ardrossan, and so began the service that continues to this day: though having passed through many different companies. The first proper pier on Arran was a wrought iron structure built at Brodick in 1872. Prior to that people had use the occasionally hazardous method of travelling from ship to shore by small boat. Boats called at almost every community on the island including Machrie, Pirnmill and Corrie, with packets also running from Ayr to Whiting Bay, Campbeltown to Blackwaterfoot and Glasgow to Brodick and Lamlash. Nowadays, there is only the main service from Ardrossan to Brodick and a seasonal service between Claonaig in Argyll and Lochranza.

Ruined croft, Glen Catacol

FROM CLACHAN TO VILLAGE

The Gaelic word for a stone is *clach*, from which develops the word for a group of stone-built houses, *clachan*. These communities, with their primitive dwellings called, on Arran, blackhouses, were based around communal agriculture. Large clachans existed at places like Thundergay, Gargadale, Blairbeg, Shannochie, Glen Catacol, the Cock, Laggan and North Glen Sannox. Agricultural reform along with the feudal attitude of aristocratic landowners brought about their demise, and a way of life was no more. These places were assigned to history and their people scattered to the winds: some to other parts of Arran, some to the mainland and, most notably, to Megantic County in Quebec, Canada. The present villages of Arran are, in the main, creations of that agricultural reform.

Sleeping Warrior profile from the North Glen Sannox Trail

Azaleas and the font, Brodick Castle Gardens

Set halfway down the east coast of Arran, Brodick, from the Norse, *brod vik*, or broad bay, was created by the 11th Duke of Hamilton in 1853, when he wished to develop the castle grounds and create a deer park. Tenants of the old village of Brodick at Cladach, just below the Castle, were re-housed in specially built workers cottages at Alma Terrace and Douglas Place. Brodick and its environs now hold over 1000 people: roughly a quarter of the island's population.

"Well if the gentry lose the land, it will only be the Lord's judgement on them for having dispossessed the people. Ah, wae's me, I hear the Duke of Hamilton's crofetrs (sic) are gaun awa' frae the Island o' Arran. Pity on us!"

James Hogg, Ettrick Shepherd,
Blackwoods Magazine of 1829

Brodick Bay from Claughlands Hill

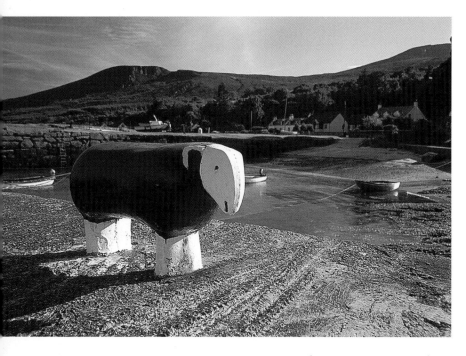

Cast iron sheep mooring, Corrie Harbour

Corrie, to the north of Brodick, gets its name from the Gaelic word for a cauldron. The word is generally used to describe a specific mountain feature. The main village now lies on the shore, though the original clachan lies higher up under Coire Lan at the foot of Goat Fell. Mentioned in records from 1449, Corrie is certainly the most picturesque of all Arran villages. Set among ancient sandstone, the main industry in the 18th century was quarrying, and piles of uncollected stones still lie on the shore. In 1886 the Corrie Parish Church was built from local red sandstone at a cost of £1,165.1s.3d. The famed Victorian writer, William Sharp was a regular visitor to the Corrie Hotel and there, in 1893, created the name Fiona – often thought of as an ancient Scottish name. Sharp thereafter famously wrote under the pseudonym, Fiona MacLeod.

Villa, Corrie

Corrie, the Sandstone Harbour

Fuchsia Cottage, Corrie

Corrie

Sannox, from the Norse, *sand vik,* or sandy bay, lies at the foot of one of the islands most dramatic views, Glen Sannox. Two hundred years ago this was one of the most populated parts of the island, with over 100 people living in the clachan of North Glen Sannox alone.

Apart from a few strung out houses the area is now mainly sheep and bracken.

Passing over the Boguille, from the Gaelic *boglach,* or marshy ground, that cuts off the previously populated Cock of Arran, the traveller will pass down Glen Chalmadale to the north of Arran and the port of Lochranza. The name combines the Gaelic word *loch* and the Norse for rowan tree river, *reynis a.* It is an ancient site, with mention of a castle as far back as 1400AD. In past times it was one of the major herring ports of the West of Scotland, employing over four hundred men. For a time it was the home of Robert Burns's Highland Mary. An ironic fact, in that Burns, who must have seen the island daily in his youth, sadly pays no mention to the island in his poetry.

Standing stones near Mossend, Brodick Country Park

On fair Lochranza streamed the early day,
Thin wreaths of cottage smoke are upward curl'd
From the lone hamlet, which her inland bay
And circling mountains sever from the world.

Lord of the Isles
Sir Walter Scott

Sannox Beach

Lochranza sunset

Lochranza Bay from An Stucan

As we move round to the northwest we come to the new settlement of Catacol, from the Norse, *katta gil;* gully of the cat. The original clachan, which lies further up Glen Catacol, is known to have existed as far back as 1445 where it is listed among the king's farms. Lord Rossmore, son-in-law of the Duke of Hamilton, evicted the population in the 1860's to make way for deer. He built a row of cottages at the present Catacol, now referred to as the Twelve Apostles. Each cottage has a unique window on the upper floor, reputed to allow the woman of the house to signal by candle to her husband fishing in Kilbrannan Sound, he being able to recognise the shape of his own peculiar window. Regardless of these niceties, the dispossessed would have none of it and removed themselves to other parts of the island.

Sculpted Rocks, Colliemore, Lochranza

Tall Ship and Ailsa Craig from Largybeg Point

Catacol Bay from Mullach Buidhe

The Twelve Apostles, Catacol

Pirnmill

Iorsa Water at Dougarie

Around 1780, following the demand for bobbins or pirns, a mill was set up at Penrioch, from the Norse practice of assigning a worth to an area of land, in this case a penny, and the Gaelic, *riabhach* meaning brindled. Although the mill ceased operations in 1840, in time A' Mhuilinn, the Mill, evolved into Pirnmill. As with most places on Arran, Pirnmill has a long association with the sea and was formerly the stopping off place on the island for the Campbeltown to Glasgow ferry. There is an amusing tale told of one Mary Sillars and her brother, Shaunie, a ghillie to the Montrose family at Dougarie, and occasional distiller of illicit spirits:

Cluster of stones on the shore, Pirate's Cove

Coirein Lochan

One day in the backend of about 90 years ago (written in 1975), the folk busy at the Banlicken still saw the Revenue cutter heave-to off the shore. A rowing boat was launched with one kilted Revenue officer aboard who came ashore. Shaunie sent the pre-arranged whistle signal to Mary in the house, who could not see what was happening, to warn her to hide the whisky that was there. She had managed to clear all evidence from downstairs by the time the officer had climbed up the footpath from the shore and was knocking at the door, ordering her to open in the name of the law. This she promptly did, and told him confidently that he could search the house. However, she had not had time to remove the ladder from the loft. When he put his foot upon it and was about to ascend, she seized a cleaver and told him in no uncertain terms in the Gaelic, that she would do him in if he dared to climb. The terrified man rushed out of the house and on returning in safety to the cutter, said, 'Nothing to report'.

History of the Villages of the Isle of Arran
Scottish Women's Rural Institute, Arran

The Gaelic word for low land by the sea is, *machair*, from which Machrie draws its name. Situated at opposite end of the String road from Brodick and populated since Stone Age times, Machrie is really a strung out community taking in Tormore, Auchengallon, Auchencar and Dougarie. Known best for its plethora of archaeological sites, Machrie also boasts a nine hole golf course on the shores of Kilbrannan Sound and the nearby King's Caves. The latter has reputed associations with Robert the Bruce and as the birthplace of the great Celtic bard, Oisin or Ossian, son of Fionn MacCuill or Fingal.

Across Machrie Moor, and under the slopes of one of Arran's five Beinn Tarsuinns, lies Shiskine. Like Machrie, Shiskine, from the Gaelic, *t-Seasgunn*, boggy place, is an extended community taking in Balmichael, Shedog, Feorline, Kilpatrick, Blackwaterfoot and Torbeg. Most of the populance live in Shedog and Blackwaterfoot. To pass through Shedog now one would scarce believe that the hamlet contained a church, school, police station, dressmaker, blacksmith, post office, two shops, as well as a mill, library, saddler, public house, hotel, doctor and undertaker.

Shishkine Golf Course

Three stones at Machrie Moor

The Doon at Drumadoon from Torr Righ Mor

Feorline was the scene of a tragedy in 1845 when the walls of the school caved in and five little girls were killed. What makes it all the more exceptional is the report that a few days before, another young girl, Maysie Bannatyne, is said to have had a premonition of five coffins laid out on the parapet of the bridge. The lass's second sight was grimly confirmed.

Running past these communities is a river that in the past would have been called, An Dhu Abhainn or Black Water. At the mouth of the stream lies Blackwaterfoot, the former port for Shiskine. Now dominated by a large hotel complex, the village is graced by a fine small harbour and, under the magnificent cliffs of the ancient fortress of Drumadoon, a popular golf course.

The various clans throughout the centuries have been associated with separate locations. For instance, Argyllshire is the home of the Campbells, M'Alisters, M'Larens, Stuarts of Appin. Dumbartonshire—M'Farlanes, M'Gregors. Perthshire—Robertsons, M'Nabs and Murrays. Inverness—Frasers, M'Leods. Banffshire—M'Kinnon, M'Intosh, M'Pherson. Buteshire—Stewarts and Bannatynes, and so on. Likewise in Arran the same names have been associated with the same district for centuries. In my own district, including Machrie, we find M'Alisters, Bannatynes, Curries, Robertsons, M'Kenzies and Murchies, and to a lesser extent the M'Masters, M'Gregors, M'Kelvies, etc. In the southend district we get the M'Kinnons, Cooks, Stuarts, M'Donalds, M'Neils. Whiting Bay—Hamiltons, M'Kelvies. Brodick with Davidsons, Fullartons. M'Brides in Lamlash. Corrie—M'Killops and Kelsos, and of course in the north end of the Island, Kerrs. Those are the names that we invariably connect with the districts just named. For instance, you won't find a Robertson or a Bannatyne in any part of the south end of the Island. Likewise, you won't find a M'Neil or Cook in Shiskine at the present day. Many of the Scottish clans never seem to have at any time a representative in Arran, viz., MacLeod, Grant, M'Farlane, M'Dougall, Cameron or M'Lean.

CLANS OF SHISKINE PAST AND PRESENT
Compiled and read by Mr. Charles Robertson, Burncliff, Shiskine,
to the Natives of Arran in Glasgow, March, 1936

The Harbour, Blackwaterfoot

In the south west corner of Arran lies Kilmorie, the Church of Mary. It comprises the hamlets of Corriecravie, Sliddery, Lagg, Kilmorie itself, Shannochie and East and West Bennan. The manse at Kilmorie was built in 1690 and, prior to its sale in the 1970s was the oldest inhabited manse in Scotland. The church holds an exceptional artefact in the form of the figurehead of the three-masted schooner, Bessie Arnold, which ran on to rocks at Sliddery in 1908. The crew, apart from the mate, perished and are buried here. The figurehead was formerly used as a gravemarker.

Clachaig is the birthplace of the scholar, Rev. William Shaw, compiler of the first Gaelic grammar and dictionary. Clachaig has also an association with Ossian where a mound is said to be his grave. It was opened in 1872 by the writer, Peter Hately Waddell, who noted that all the dimensions of the tomb followed a mathematical accuracy, but no other significant remains were discovered:

No trace of anything else, monumental or other, on the most careful scrutiny, being found, the soil was again filled in and the tombstone replaced reverentially as before.

Ossian and the Clyde
Peter Hately Waddell

Corriecravie

Kildonan is named after St Donan, a follower of Columba, who is purported to have arrived on Arran in the 6th century, and is said to be buried on Kildonan Farm, where lie the foundations of an early chapel. That there are place names dedicated to those who could never have visited the island such as Kilpatrick, Kilmichael or Kilbride means neither that Donan arrived or did not, but it is quite possible. Donan went on to be abbot of the monastery on Eigg and in 616AD was there martyred.

Kildonan, Pladda and Ailsa Craig from Dippen Fort

The most significant landmark at Kildonan is the castle. Set on a low cliff, it was almost certainly fortified to the landward side by a ditch. Its date of structure is unknown but is mentioned in a medieval record of 1406 when Robert III granted it to a Stewart, a son not by his wife.

Continuing the circumnavigation of the island in an anti-clockwise direction, or widdershins, as the Celts say, we come to Whiting Bay on the south east of Arran. Known in Gaelic as Am Bagh, The Bay, the area originally consisted of the districts of North, Mid and South Kiscadale, King's Cross, Auchencairn, Sandbraes, Largiemohr, Largiemeanoch and Largiebeag. Although the Vikingr claimed overlordship of Arran their presence is not greatly marked on the island. However, there is a significant Vikingr fort and boat burial site at King's Cross at the north end of Whiting Bay. The area hosts other significant archaeological sites, including the Giant's Graves at the southern end of the village. This cluster of stones is of the type known as a Neolithic chambered cairn, of which Arran has some twenty-three sites.

Kildonan Castle

Standing Stones at Largybeg Point

Whiting Bay from the Giant's Grave

Lamlash from the pier

On the road back to Brodick lies Lamlash. Like most of Arran's communities it is strung out over a great distance. Variously called Loch an Eilan, Kilbride or Kirktoun, the village has been in existence since at least the 14th century. The remains of a chapel dating from that time, and dedicated to St Bride, can be found in the Kilbride burial ground. Because of the shelter afforded by Holy Island, Lamlash Bay has long been a harbour for fleets of ships: from the Fleet of Hakon in the 13th century to the North Atlantic fleets in both World Wars. The humble township has played host to King Hakon and King George VI, not to mention one of the great heroes of the 20th century, Winston Churchill. Lamlash also hosts The Isle of Arran War Memorial Hospital and Arran High School, both of which serve the entire island. It is also the resting-place of seventeen American World War II pilots whose plane crashed into the Arran during bad weather - one of the highest casualties of pilots in a single incident ever recorded

Travelling the magnificent highways and byways of Arran, one might notice that the island's bridges are built on a bend in the road. It is well enough known that a witch will not cross running water, but neither could they traverse a bend in the road. Nothing like making sure.

Lamlash from Dunan Beag

Three geese at Kildonan Shore

FIN, WING, HOOF AND LEAF

With an enormous variety of habitats, Arran is the proverbial birdwatcher's paradise. The surrounding sea is home to the usual variety of gulls, though the larger breeds tend to nest on moorland. Gannets from Ailsa Craig can be seen making their spectacular dives as well as guillemot, shag and cormorant. Ducks such as the red-breasted merganser, shellduck and eider can be found scuttering noisily over the wavetops. You will find a proliferation of waders, dunlin, sanderling, turnstone, oyster catcher and redshank on the shoreline and Jackdaw, kestrel, peregrine and rock dove on the sea cliffs. Chaffinch, starling, thrush and robin, as well as rock pippit, wagtail, yellowhammer and dunnock, along with siskin, blue and great tit, treecreeper, goldcrest wren, pigeon and woodcock inhabit forest and farm. Skylark, ring ousel, meadow pippit, grouse, raven, curlew, buzzard and the magnificent hen harrier and golden eagle can be found on moor and mountain.

Rock Pippit and Ailsa Craig, Kildonan

Seals, Brodick Bay

Plankton and numerous species of fish, including scallop, prawn, plaice, cod monkfish skate and haddock, inhabit the waters of Kilbrannan Sound and the Firth of Clyde, providing a ready larder for seabirds, porpoise, basking shark and seal. Rabbit, hare, badger, hedgehog, shrew, mouse and vole can be found onshore, but no stoat, weasel or fox, though, in recent times, the otter has made a comeback. Red squirrel dwell in the woodlands and adder and red deer on the mountains. Surprisingly, the island has toads, but no frogs.

The Beach at Drumadoon Point

Although the west of Arran is only around twelve miles from the east coast, the rainfall is dramatically less, with an annual level of around 46 inches at Dougarie and 70 inches at Brodick. The generally mild and damp climate is a haven for flora of all descriptions. Even at Christmas time there are over 50 species of wild flower in bloom: the most obvious of these being gorse or whin. Along the shoreline is thrift, sea campion and navelwort, cranesbill and butterburr, sandwart, silverweed and searocket. Woodlands consist of Oak, ash, beech, hazel, alder, birch and rowan, of which there is a species known only to Arran. In these woodlands you will find primrose, bluebell, wood anemone and golden saxifrage. Along roadways are celandine, stitchwort, red campion and honeysuckle. On the bogland you will find yellow iris, bogbean, meadowsweet, ragwort and bog cotton and the beautifully scented, bog myrtle. The glens and mountains can seem lacking in colour until you peer closer and find - besides bracken, heather and purple mountain grass - tormentil, milkwort, carnivorous sundew and starry saxifrage. Although 90 percent of flowering plants on Arran are white, colours vary as we move through the seasons: yellow to white, red, purple then back to yellow. Because of the mild climate Arran is the home for some exotic plants including the Cardyline Palm, brought over by the eminent horticulturalist, David Landsborough.

Wildflower meadow, Largybeg

South shore, Whiting Bay

Brodick Castle Gardens

Two Ashes, Glen Catacol

Gate to the Glen, Lochranza (1987)

MYTH, LEGEND AND FOLKLORE

Inevitably, Arran tends to share its myth, legend and folklore with that of the West Highlands. Undoubtedly it was place loved by the Celts. In Irish legend it is called, Emain Abhlach, the Land of Apples, and is the equivalent of Avalon in British mythology. That it has associations with Finn and Ossian is without doubt, and figures in the great work of Ossianic poetry. In his Tales of the West Highlands, J.F.Campbell says:

I may add, that at this day (1862) men still point out Dun Finn in Arran and explain "Ar-ainn" to mean Ar-fhinn, Fin's land

There are a few unusual facts about Arran that may rightly come under the heading of modern folklore: The house subject to the least sunshine in the British Isles is at Lochranza and, relative to the size of the community, *The Arran Banner* has the highest circulation of any newspaper. It is the only place in Britain where the beaches and water around the island do not belong to the crown: they are in fact, the property of Arran Estates.

Sunlight, Claughlands Forest

There are a few tales that are known to be specific to the island. One lovely tale of the fairy folk was told to Alexander Carmichael, compiler of the magnificent Carmina Gadelica:

Donald Macalastair, seventy-nine years of age, crofter, Druim-a-ghinnir, Arran, told me, in the year 1895, the following story in Gaelic :—' The fairies were dwelling in the knoll, and they had a near neighbour who used to visit them in their home. The man used to observe the ways of the fairies and to do as they did. The fairies took a journey upon them to go to Ireland, and the man took upon him to go with them. Every single fairy of them caught a ragwort and went astride it, and they were pell-mell, every knee of them across the Irish Ocean in an instant, and across the Irish Ocean was the man after them, astride a ragwort like one of themselves. A little wee tiny fairy shouted and asked were they all ready, and all the others replied that they were, and the little fairy called out :—

Going across in my haste,
On the crests of the waves,
To Ireland.

Standing stone at start of walk, Claughlands Hill

"Follow me," said the king of the fairies, and away they went across the Irish Ocean, every mother's son of them astride his ragwort. Macuga (Cook) did not know on earth how he would return to his native land, but he leapt upon the ragwort as he saw the fairies do, and he called as he heard them call, and in an instant he was back in Arran. But he had got enough of the fairies on this trip itself, and he never went with them again.'

Waterfall and stone, Glen Rosa

Lochranza Bay from Newton Point

Arran Ferry approaches Ardrossan

THE 21ST CENTURY

So, what of Arran in the 21st century? Without doubt, tourism is the lifeblood of the island. Around quarter of a million people visit in any given year: from the early arrival of often-spotted geology student, to the summer influx of visitors on the Calmac ferry out of Ardrossan. Some come for a day's climbing before catching the last boat back, some on bicycles for a leisurely two-wheeled tour and some by car, occasionally with a caravan tacked to the back. In consequence the island has many hotels, campsites, bed and breakfast accommodation and a seemingly endless choice of holiday homes.

It is also a place of refuge for many: people who have visited and stayed. In truth, going back far enough, everyone is a settler or the descendant of one.

Loch Iorsa

Lamlash from the coast road

Sunset over Arran from Adrossan Ferry

While tourism might dominate the economy it is by no means the sole provider. Agriculture is strong, with the raising of beef cattle, sheep and dairy cattle. The latter supplying the creamery at Torrylin, where an award winning cheese is manufactured and exported worldwide. To go along with your cheese you might like to try some of Arran's very own mustard manufactured at Lamlash, and to wash it down a dram from the distillery at Lochranza or Arran Ale from Cladach Brewery. On your way you might pick up some strange and exotic scents coming from the island's fastest growing industry at Home Farm, Brodick where an assortment of aromatic toiletries are manufactured.

Although suffering a set-back in the so-called 'banana wars' between the USA and the EU, the company has had an exponential growth in the last few years

What the future holds for Arran is in the stars, but it is certain that the island will never cease to be a place of wonder and intrigue. Yes! Arran is a thoroughly unique and extraordinary place indeed. In the words of William Sharp:

See Naples and die: – unless you have not yet seen Arran

Seal basking on rock at Kildonan

BIBLIOGRAPHY
AND RECOMMENDED READING
ON ARRAN

Balfour, J.A.   *The Book of Arran Vol I*

Boyle, Andrew   *Pictorial History of Arran (Alloway Publishing)*

Campbell J.F.   *Popular Tales of the West Highlands (Wildwood House)*

Carmichael, Alexander   *Carmina Gadelica*

Church, T. & Smith T.   *The Arran Flora (Arran Natural History Society)*

Cancy, Thomas Owen   *The Triumph Tree (Cannongate Classics)*

Faihurst, Horace   *Exploring Arran's Past*

Fraser, Ian A.   *The Place-Names of Arran*

Gemmell, Alistair   *Discovering Arran (John Donald)*

McCrorie, Ian   *The Sea Routes to Arran (Calmac)*

MacKenzie, W.M.   *The Book of Arran Vol II*

McLaughlin, Bill   *Molaise of Arran (W.J. McLaughlin)*

McLellan, Rober   *The Isle of Arran (David and Charles)*

Mitchell-Luker B.   *Arran Bus Book (Kilbrannan Press)*

Rhead, John & Snow Philip   *Birds of Arran (Saker Press)*

Scottish Natural Heritage   *Arran and the Clyde Islands (S.N.H.)*

S.W.R.I. (Arran Federation)   *History of the Villages of the Isle of Arran*

Thompson, Ruth & Allan   *The Milestones of Arran*

Whyte, Hamish (Editor)   *An Arran Anthology (Mercat Press)*

KEY GAELIC AND NORSE WORDS FOUND ON ARRAN:

Abhainn	river		*Monaidh*	moor
Achadh	field		*Mullaich*	summit
Aird	headland		*Mhor*	big
Allt	stream		*Puill*	pool
Ard	high		*Righ*	king
Baille	township		*Ruabh*	red
Ban	fair		*Sliabh*	moor
Beag	small		*Srath*	valley
Beinn	mountain		*Suidhe*	seat
Breac	speckled		*Tigh*	house
Cill	church		*Torr*	mound
Coille	wood		*Tullach*	hill
Clach	stone		*Uisge*	water
Cnoc	hill			
Dhu	black		*A*	river
Druim	ridge		*Askr ash*	tree
Eilean	island		*Dalr*	valley
Fionn	fair or white			
Garbh	rough		*Fjall*	mountain
Gleann	valley		*Gil*	ravine
Gobhar	goat		*Vik*	bay
Iolaire	eagle			
Loch	lake			
Machrach	low-lying plain			
Mara	sea			
Meall	hill			